Black, White and Tan

Written by: Nicole C Mullen   Illustrated By: Tom Bancroft & Rob Corley

Black, White and Tan

Published by: Mullenville Media
Web Address: www.nicolecmullen.com
ISBN: 13 Number: 978-0-9816285-1-6

Written by: Nicole C Mullen
Illustrated By: Tom Bancroft & Rob Corley for funnypages Productions
Based on the Song "Black White and Tan" (Nicole C. Mullen/David Mullen)
from the album Nicole C. Mullen (2000)

Cover Design & Art Direction: funnypages Productions www.funnypagesprod.com

Printed In Mexico

Hi my name is lil' Jas.

I live in a big house full of love,

With my mom, dad, and three brothers.

We all look a little different,

But we are the same family.

We are black, white and tan,

Like a human rainbow,

And we love each other very much.

When God made me,

He gave me big brown eyes,

And dark wavy hair.

Sometimes it is very curly

And sometimes I like to wear it straight.

He also gave me tan skin.

It is the color of coffee

Mixed with cream,

A shade of honey,

Kissed by the sun.

And This is my mom. I think she is very pretty.

Her hair is dark and curly, and her skin is a beautiful shade of brown.

Brown like coffee...

... or even sweet maple syrup.

... or yummy chocolate cake...

They say that she is black,

But she is not the color of night,

Not the color of black.

She is brown,

She is black,

And love is black, white and tan.

This is my dad. He loves playing football with my three brothers,

And telling silly jokes to make us all laugh.

He has light brown,

Straight hair,

And his skin is the color

Of peaches with cream,

Or beige with rosey cheeks.

They say that he is white,

But he is not the color of paper,

Not the color of white.

He is beige,

He is white,

And love is black, white and tan.

These are my brothers,

Two of them have dark hair

And brown skin like hot chocolate,

The same as my mom.

The other one has tan skin and wavy hair just like me.

We have lots of fun, singing and dancing together,

Or hanging out with our friends.

My brothers also love playing video games,

Reading books and helping my dad in the yard.

This is how it is for us.

We are different,

And we are the same.

We are family

And love is black white and tan.

My mom and dad said that God's family is a lot like ours.

Some have brown skin...

... some have cream skin...

.... some have tan skin..

Different people,

Of all colors, shapes and sizes.

Together we make a human rainbow,

Because we are all

From the same family.

I like the colors that I see,

And I love being ME!

Together we are beautiful!

Because love is black, white and tan.